Bramble
The Symbol of the Purity
of the Virgin Mary

Butterfly
The Symbol of Resurrection

Random Egyptian Images

Lamb
The Symbol of Jesus

Holly
The Symbol of Christ's
Crown of Thorns

Bee
The Symbol of the Activity, Diligence,
Work, and Good Order

Stag *Bull*
Symbol... Religi...

Water
Cleansing, Purifying, and Baptism

Dolphin
The Symbol of Salvation

Fish
The Symbol of Jesus

Hare
...bolizes the men who cut their
...n in Christ and his passion

Bulrush
The Symbol of Faithful
Multitudes of the Church

Peacock
The Symbol of Immortality

Spider
The Symbol of Malice
of Evil-Doers

The Symbol of Passion and
Peter's Denial of Christ

Cypress
The Symbol of Death

Ram
The Symbol of Jesus

Butterfly
The Symbol of Resurrection

Jesus Nazarenus Rex Judaeorum
INRI
Jesus of Nazareth, King of Jews

Birds
The Symbol of the
Winged Soul

Goat
The Symbol of the
Last Judgment

This book belongs to:

_____

Tommy NELSON

Journey, Easter Journey!

by **Dandi Daley Mackall**
Illustrations by **Gene Barretta**

www.tommynelson.com

A Division of Thomas Nelson, Inc.
www.ThomasNelson.com

Published in Nashville, Tennessee, by Tommy Nelson®, a Division of Thomas Nelson, Inc.

ISBN 1-4003-0373-7

Printed in Colombia
04 05 06 07 BVG 5 4 3 2 1

Dedication

For Katelyn Daley Brigmon—
Welcome to the beginning of your "Journey" with Jesus.
—Dandi

Thank you, Joan, for all the Christian symbols.
Thank you, Pastor Steve, for the informative conversations.
And thank you, Debbie, for Isaiah.

Leslie, I have a life that I love
because I have a wife that I love.
—G

Jesus on a journey, ending down in Bethlehem,
Left his home in heaven to live a while on Earth.
Mary and her Joseph journey up from Nazareth,
All the way to Bethlehem, a stable for the birth.

Journey, journey, Jesus! Jesus took a journey,
Whirling past the angel wings.
Listen as the angel sings,
"Here he comes! The King of Kings!"
Journey, journey on!

Jesus on a journey.
    Donkeys running—*clip, clip clop!*
Bouncing Baby Jesus,
    safe on Mary's lap.
Racing fast to Egypt,
    fleeing from the bad, bad king.
Miles and miles and miles to go
    before he takes a nap!

Journey, journey, Jesus! Jesus took a journey,
Trotting through the Holy Land,
Guided by God's loving hand,
Crossed the desert through the sand.
Journey, journey on!

Jesus on a journey, journeys back to Nazareth,
Working as a carpenter, growing big and strong.
Hammer, hammer, *bang, bang!* Building in his father's shop,
Reading Scripture, trusting God, knowing right from wrong.

Journey, journey, Jesus! Jesus took a journey,
Journeyed home to Galilee,
Grew up with his family,
Worked in his community.
Journey, journey on!

Jesus on a journey,
    spreading God the Father's love,
Getting out the Good News
    to all of Galilee!
Journey in a fishing boat,
    teaching his disciples,
Quieting the winds and waves
    in a storm at sea.

Journey, journey, Jesus! Jesus took a journey.
He's the Way, the Truth, the Light!
On a wild and stormy night,
Making everything all right.
Journey, journey on!

Jesus on a journey, sad and lonely journey,
Hardest journey in the world, in all of history.
Marching through the city, heading up to Calvary,
On the cross was crucified. He died for you and me.

Journey, journey, Jesus! Jesus took a journey,
All alone, without a friend,
Knew what lay around the bend.
Could this be the journey's end?
Journey, journey on!

Jesus on a journey,
    carried to a cold, dark cave,
Soldiers guarding Jesus,
    who's left inside the tomb.
Early Easter morning,
    women come to mourn his death,
But the stone is rolled away
    from the empty room!

Journey, journey, Jesus! Jesus took a journey!
Paid a debt he didn't owe—
Women searching high and low—
Where *is* Jesus? Do *you* know?
Journey, journey on!

Jesus on a journey, left the tomb and rose again!
Happy Easter morning! Proof that Jesus lives!
Hallelujah, Savior! Jesus rose on Easter Day!
Best of all the miracles, life that Jesus gives!

Journey, journey, Jesus! Jesus took a journey.
Back to heaven—all is new!
Easter's journey was for *you!*
Someday, we can journey, too.
Journey, journey on!

Bramble

The Symbol of the Purity of the Virgin Mary

Butterfly

The Symbol of Resurrection

Random Egyptian Images

Lamb

The Symbol of Jesus

Holly

The Symbol of Christ's Crown of Thorns

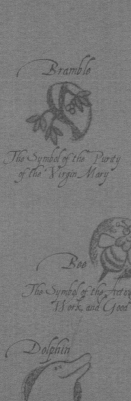

Bee

The Symbol of the Activity, Diligence, Work, and Good Order

Stag

Symbolizes Piety and Religious Aspiration

Bull

Brute Strength

Water

Cleansing, Purifying, and Baptism

Dolphin

The Symbol of Salvation

Fish

The Symbol of Jesus

Pomegranate

The Symbol of the Church, the unity of All the Seeds in one Fruit

Hare

Symbolizes the Men Who Put Their Salvation in Christ and His Passion

Bulrush

The Symbol of Faithful Multitudes of the Church

Peacock

The Symbol of Immortality

Spider

The Symbol of Malice of Cool Doors

Cock

The Symbol of Passion and Peter's Denial of Christ

Cypress

The Symbol of Death

Ram

The Symbol of Jesus

Butterfly

The Symbol of Resurrection

Jesus Nazarenus Rex Judaeorum

I.N.R.I.

Jesus of Nazareth, King of Jews

Birds

The Symbol of the Winged Soul

Goat

The Symbol of the Last Judgment